The Melancholy Of Life

Lila Prasad Sharma

BookLeaf Publishing
India | USA | UK

Made with ❤ on the BookLeaf Publishing Platform
www.bookleafpub.in
www.bookleafpub.com

Dedication

"This is for those —
Who think,
Who feel,
Who question,
Who doubt,
Who remember and
Who seek,
The endlessness of life."

Preface

I wrote this book as a personal remembrance, for myself and my future self. This book is not just a collection of poems, but a reflection of how I think and feel.

Perhaps one of these lines will stir a thought or feeling within you—one you have never known before. Through these poems, I want you to question the unquestionable, see the unseen, feel the unfelt, and live the unliveable.

This book explores themes of illusion, unseen perspectives, nihilism, and the tragedies of life. These words may hold a meaning different from what I intended, but that is the beauty of language and the human mind—to perceive what others overlook and to feel what others ignore.

If my poems make you pause, think, doubt, or question—even for a brief moment—then they have served their purpose.

Now, this book belongs to you—a part of me that you now carry. May these words guide you and help you grow into something more than you were before.

Acknowledgements

To everyone who made this book possible—my friends, my family, the trees, the leaves, the flowers, the river, the ocean, the clouds, the rain, the bees, the wind, the sound, the touch, the imagination, the shadow, the moon, and the sky—I thank you.

This book would not be complete without my greatest teachers—my mother and father. One who taught me to hold the pencil, the other who inspired me to write.

And finally, to you—thank you for choosing to read this book, for giving my words a place to exist beyond me, and for making them immortal.

1. Last Flight

Stepped in this ruthless world,
Naked and afraid only to suffer in silence.
She weeps in sorrow to a deaf crowd,
Covering their ears to the side.

With no one to listen to her cry,
She looks at others for hope.
But the only sight she sees,
Are backs turned away from her.

She thinks, what did she do to deserve this,
Was merely being born in this place enough?
She closes her eyes, the only other sound she hears
Are those of other women crying.

Opening her eyes, through the mist it appears—
A silver horse, shimmering like moonlight on the sea.
With wings of silver and powerful flight,
Carries her to the golden sky.

2. Final Walk

"You are a man!" said the society,
Yet, the words felt hollow in his hands.
He looked into his father's eyes
—Saw only himself.

Upon walking a few steps,
He stepped on a thorn.
Without a cry, without a pause, he kept walking.
For he was a man of society.

He found someone walking ahead,
Called out "Hey!", for he could not bear the pain
anymore.
The man turned, met his gaze,
Catching a breath he said, "Hey," and kept walking.

With no one to hear his silent cries,
He kept on walking until at last he fell.
Hearing the sound of his fall, they came like vultures,
Not to help, but to mock, to sneer, to pick at his remains.

Laughter echoed where mercy should have been,
But when they pulled him up, they found only a child,
Cradled in soft white feathers, eyes shut to the world.

3. Flower and Leaf

Glimmering with beauty, the flower stands atop,
Only to be plucked by romantic hands.
The bees kiss the flowers goodbye,
Then move on, seeking more.

Looking plain and green, the leaves
Have no beauty of their own.
No hands to touch them,
No bees to kiss goodbye.

With a bit of sadness and pain,
The leaves long to be seen.
They wait and wait,
Only to dry and fall, broken on the ground.

The flowers long for the leaf's endless days,
To live, not fade, and die in peace.
The leaves wish for the beauty of a flower,
Just to feel the slightest touch of love.

The flowers know they are loved only for appearances,
Left to be plucked and forgotten.
Their beauty does not last long,
All that remains is vase loneliness.

The leaves have a long life,
But no admiration for their beauty or bravery in the
wind.
All they ever feel are raindrops,
A love that never stays.

The flowers wish to be seen as they are,
Not left with the ache of ornamental grief.
The leaves wish to feel love's gentle touch,
Not left to wither, dry, and fall.

Both, burdened by their quiet grief,
Are left to fade in sorrow.

4. Wind

From high to low, it wanders,
Gently touching every soul.
With a gentle touch and frail move,
Wanders the world in a rhythmic blue.

With the first fire, it witnessed
The dawn of humanity.
Slowly leaving the dark cave,
Humans explored.

Lifting birds and scattering leaves,
Filled the sails of the brave explorers.
On the endless horizon, it pushed forward.
Leaving the cries of those left behind.

It watched two brothers soar the sky.
Wooden wings trembling in the air.
But this time, it did not resist,
but gave a gentle push to move forward.

As men lost their humanity,
the wind became helpless.
Heavy with smoke, thick with cries,
carried the weight of shattered lives.

Unseen waves now it carries,
for now, it sees the beginning of digital age.
Carrying the voices of joy and sadness,
it traverses around the world.

Slowly darkening, tainted with poison,
the wind that once gave life now turns bitter.
For humans forgot the wind,
that once kissed their weary cheeks.

5. I Wish I Was

I wish I was a mountain,
Standing strong and deep.
Touching the sky,
Shaping the whole world.

I wish I was a river,
Always moving, fearless, with no memories of the past.
But still giving life and carrying people
To their final destination.

I wish I was a tree, giving life,
Asking nothing in return.
With branches reaching the sky,
And leaves waving goodbye.

I wish I was a cloud,
Drifting endlessly in the vastness of sky.
Quenching the thirst of others
And slowly losing myself in return.

I wish I was the Wind,
Carrying joy and laughter everywhere.
Reminding any soul I touch
About their past endeavours.

I wish I was a Star,
Unreachable, but guiding everyone through their life.
Holding the mystery of the universe,
Slowly fading into infinite darkness.

I wish to be everything there is,
Feel everything there is,
And not get lost in this world,
As everyone before me has.

6. Old Age

Wrinkled cheeks, silver threads of hair.
Teeth now falling, a voice grown weak,
Weakening hands and trembling legs,
Fading vision, a dimming gaze.

My prime, once bright, now fades with time.
Loneliness getting stronger,
Words spoken getting smaller.
And the whole world getting taller

A stride once effortless and free,
Now takes five slow steps from me.
Time bends the path, reshapes the mile,
What once took a stride now takes a while.

My heart sinks remembering my past,
My endeavour, my struggle, my love.
Will they remember me when I'm gone,
Or fade my name as dusk moves on?

It seems my time has come,
Am I prepared, am I ready?
I would not know, for I have become too old,
And the world seems to have grown cold.

7. In Search of God

God must find it strange,
What His creation has become.
Once soul of purest white,
Now reshaped in countless moulds.

He remembers sculpting us,
With his own bare hands.
A masterpiece of beauty and bright,
Now a vessel of greed and fright.

But what He finds most strange of all—
Is how we lost humanity in search of Him.
How we seek Him in temples of stone,
Yet fail to hear Him whisper when alone.

He fears we may never find Him
and even if we do—
We may not recognise Him,
For the countless image we have made of Him.

8. I Do Not Know

Whom to share my sorrow, whom to share my joy?
They listen, but do they truly hear?

Whom to lay my head upon, whom to offer my
shoulder?
It is uncertain—are we all searching for the same?

Whom to cry for help, whom to give help?
We cry together, but none ask for help.

Whom to worship, whom to pray?
A name, a stone—or something beyond?

Whom to show my kindness, whom to show my love?
Do we love because we want to be loved, or because we
want to love?

Whom to fear, whom to trust?
Do I fear the unknown and trust the already known?
But how do I know I can trust the known and fear the

unknown?

Whom to forgive, whom to remember?
Can we forgive without remembering? Or do we
remember because we have forgiven?

I do not know.
But what I do know is, no one truly knows.

9. A Beautiful Song

A beautiful song is sung
To an audience that cannot hear.

A cry for help
To an audience that only laughs.

A majestic dance
To an audience that cannot see.

A masterpiece of color
To an audience that sees only grey.

A poem full of meaning
To an audience that cannot read.

Humanity
To an audience that has none.

And yet, I still sing, I still dance, I still paint—
For I am both the audience and the performer.

10. In The Hands Of Time

The blooming flower bud,
Slowly starts to wrinkle,
Once a thing of beauty,
Now fading into dust.

A child with glowing eyes,
Gazes at the stars.
Seeking his place in the world,
Only to find himself at its end.

A man who once chased glory,
Sees his end near.
All that remains —
A shattered ego and silver strands.

For time is the ultimate fate,
And even the greatest empires crumble to dust.
Hence, have no fear—
For we all share the same fate in the hands of time.

11. Cage

With no say, no choice,,
Thrown in this world without voice.
Naked and afraid,
Trapped in a frail body.

A prisoner to your own body,
Like a bird in a cage inside a forrest.
There is no escape from here,
The only escape is death itself.

A journey of loneliness and joy,
Gathering people for funeral.
For when death comes,
The only thing left is dust and fading memory.

12. Company Of A Wolf

It's a dark and lonely road,
No light to guide me—only endless black.
No path before me,
Only shadows, darker than night.

A white wolf trails behind me,
Whimpering, afraid of the dark.
He looks at me, ears pressed tight,
I am as still as him.

He knows my fear for him,
So he keeps his distance, yet stays near.
I continue walking forward,
And he follows me behind.

The only light guiding us,
Are the scattered stars above.
A cold breeze brushes my skin.
My friend stops, whimpers, then follows again.

And when the golden light of morning bleeds into the
sky.
I turn to look for my friend—but he is not there.
I think of him for a moment,
I exhale. Relieved— or sad, perhaps.

13. The Last Leaf

A gentle touch of wind gives him a shake,
A hollow feeling stirs him awake.
He clings between life and death,
Barely holding on to the branch.

Raindrops begin to fall,
He thinks — this is it.
He cannot hold much longer,
Tears start trailing down him.

In the end rain surrenders before his will.
How long can he hold, he thinks.
For fall is his unkind fate.
A feeling of deep sorrow weighs him.

He begins remembering,
Life unfolding before him.
How a small bird with tiny wings,
Took first flight in the endless sky.

He remembers,
How two birds in their old age,
Slowly died in each others arms.
With no eyes to mourn their death.

He remembers,
The first time he saw sunrise,
The golden flames reaching the infinity,
A gentle wind touching his cheeks.

He remembers,
When he saw himself turning brown,
The setting of his final fate.
When he, finally understood himself.

Now, the time is near for him to leave.
The sun rises in golden ocean of clouds.
A final breeze kisses his green body,
And he lets go—
Drifting into the sky he once admired—A final breath of
freedom.

14. I, Me and Him

I look at the mirror,
See a familiar face.
He is dressed like me,
Moving like me,
Looking right back at me.

Who am I? I wonder.
Am I the one who is looking at him?
Or am I the one —
Looking at me?

What is the difference between him and me?
He looks just like me, so he must be me.
But who is real—him, or me?
I try to find myself.

Is he wondering the same thing as I?
Trying to find himself from behind the mirror.
Or does he think for himself?
Thinking of something rather different than me.

When I am not looking,
Does he look at me?
Or does he look away, just like I do?
I don't know, and neither does he.

If I die, will he be still alive?
Or, die along with me?
If we are the same then,
How does we look at each other differently?

If we are not the same then,
why does he move as I move and feel as I feel?
If I shatter the mirror, who truly breaks—
I, Me, or Him?

15. Shadow

It follows you from the first light,
Through childhood's journey to the end of night.
It walks with you all the places,
Watching you behind all faces.

With neither rest nor tire,
Through icy cold winter and raging fire.
Bound to you till eternity,
A simple life of fate and destiny.

And when at last you meet the end,
It, too must lose its final mend.
With no whisper or story,
It is left with you to bury.

16. Between Time And Death

It watches me on my every move,
I cannot hide from it or run from it.
It talks to me about my past, present and future,
My birth and my end.

I try to reach it,
But before I can touch it, slips away.
It is slow when I am suffering,
And fast when I am loved.

I do not truly understand it,
Is it my friend or foe?
Or perhaps both?
I do not know.

It whispers to me sometimes,
In moments of sorrow and stolen breath.
Tells me how it is inevitable,
Tells me how it is my ultimate destiny.

I do not know how I feel,
For I have known death to be my ultimate destiny.
Is it that time speaks to us through death?
Or is death itself time?

17. Unseen Thread

Thread unseen pulls me,
Through my darkest fear and joyous mood.
It remains unseen, yet pulls me within,
For I walk, holding an unknown hand.

A river flowing down a mountain,
Has no fixed path, no chosen walk.
Yet, it walks the longest of path,
and carves the hardest of mountains.

As the river reaches us,
It is given a name, a name it deserves.
To whom do we give a name?
The river of water or the fate which made the river great.

Like the river, my path remains unseen,,
Yet, I walk unknown of my journey.
Do I walk this journey,
Or does fate walk me?

18. Moon

A pale silver eye in the midnight sky,
Watching over us in darkest of night.
He is silent, never makes a sound but,
Always watching and guiding through the night.

A symbol of beauty and perfection,
With imperfection in him.
He has witnessed countless birth, death,
murder and treachery but, remains silent.

19. The Death

He gives meaning to our life,
Some fear him, others dare to face him.
Some try to run away and some try to run towards,
And some merely wait for his warm embrace.

What is rich and poor, beautiful and ugly,
Fat and thin, short and tall to death.
For everyone is equal in the hands of death,
No saint, no sinner, No child, No mother only echoes of
life.

The ultimate truth and law of life,
Equal and fair,
Some might say otherwise,
For some death is freedom and for some it is void.

Death—the only meaningful event,
In this short dream we call life.
For he is the question and the answer,
To the unknown purpose of life.

20. Someone Somewhere

Someone somewhere lost his dearest friend,
Someone somewhere found a bond that won't end.
Someone somewhere had his freedom denied,
Someone somewhere seeks where meaning resides.

Someone somewhere sold his truthful voice,
Someone somewhere made his final choice.
Someone somewhere let go of his life,
Someone somewhere saw his afterlife.

Someone somewhere lost her reason to live,
Someone somewhere found new strength to give.
Someone somewhere took his final breath,
Someone somewhere questioned the meaning of death.

Someone somewhere lost her battle,
Someone somewhere rose through the rattle.
Someone somewhere had no more tears to cry,
Someone somewhere found his battle cry.

21. Freedom

The bird seems to be free,
Roaming freely in endless hush.
For it too is bound to the sky,
By a invisible thread pulling it down.

A river too seems free,
Carves it's own path, marks it's own way.
For it too is bound to Earth,
In a long journey through cycle of death and rebirth.

Clouds too seems free,
Roams around the sky high, endless and free.
But, it too must rain and fall to Earth,
And again begin it's journey to the oceans.

We too seem free,
We think what we think and feel what we feel.
But, do we think our own and feel what is our own?
Are we not bound, like all before? Destined to dust—
forevermore?

* 9 7 8 9 3 6 9 5 4 5 0 0 1 *